Tracing fingerprints

A poetry collection

With thanks to Jo, my mum and her tireless mentoring, to David and his loving support, and Sharon for her generous help (again!) and all my family and friends for just being there.

'And all things, whatsoever ye shall ask in prayer, believing, ye shall receive.' St Matthew 21 22

Other books: let's make tea out of roses, Roses in the tea caddy Tea and afternoon roses, Echoes of faith One more daisy 'til i love you, Salt in the wound.

Weaving in and out of challenges and hopes and fears I hope the reader will find some elucidating words and meaning in this collection of poems.

'And in sizzling swarms like clotted fire honey glistens in my russet jaw'

From Clouds of honey

Enjoy the read,

Claire

Cover design by the author

Instagram: @everywordisamemory(Claire Gibson./ Booth)

Editor Sharon Andrews Instagram: @inksomnia_poetry (also a poetess)

GREETINGS CARDS ALSO AVAILABLE FROM CLAIRE email boothclaire040@gmail.com

Contents

Daffodil 6

Revelation of daffodils 7

River 9

Scratched by shadow 10

In the shadow of light 11

Stars of gold 12

Summers and winters 13

The muse is singing 14

The revelation of spring 15

Leaves 17

Sea 18

In Rows 19

Tide 23

Watch 24

Berry 26

World 28

As the lilac wanes 29

Blizzards 30

Breathing light...31

Clouds of honey 33

Daffodil

In between the daffodils
Came strips of shadow on the earth,
Striped like blue swallows
Reaching for spring.

And in the nests
Where growing is done
The simple tiny birds' flying
Has just begun,
Where colours fade
One by one into shadow striped in blue.

And the daffodil thrills
As light like bells decorates her bloom.

Revelation of daffodils

Breathing their birth
Into the secretive earth
The winter bulbs
Move the crumbs of soil
In a slow march
From sleepy slumber
To the cockerel of dawn.

The covered whispers,
Bloated and bobbing,
Chuckle in the silver stones of sod.

Reverberating tiny sounds,
Blind bandits of the gritty ground
Sing like sailors to the newborn air.

And who could tell which starlit bloom
Would flower first,
Which brimming bud
Would open last?
And when the echo back to root
Plainly stoops in cowered hood?
Who can tell which leaf will fold
And when the withered stem will take hold?

But surely as new shoots are driven
And the daffodil blurs in my vision
Every colour that in her petals glisten
Must be made from a chorus of angels
In unison.

River

As I watch the water ebb
Across a cloudy stream
Throwing lily shadows
Across the pools of pain
How small are the discs blown in blue
From the fish's ringlet lips,
And how this 'water village' skips,
How it holds my mind,
My wits.

And in the bubbling gleeful stream
Where all flows noiseless, gold and green
A marina river new does gleam
Across a pebble bridge.

Away she goes
The river flows
Towards a brightened sea
And silky as the wind that blows
Her motion gallops free.

Scratched by shadow

The trees
Through lacy leaves
Like ink blots of sky
Dally with the breeze.

Synchronised shadows leap
Like dungeons in my sleep.
Cold lies like rain in white.

All the patterns in my brain
Call out
To each tree
Petticoated like fractures of pain
Drizzling away,
Drizzling away
As the sky turns palpably grey
In the sleepful night.

In the shadow of light

This dance is in shadow
Flickering between the hazelnuts and leaves.

The birds did not sing today,
I did not hear the trumpets play.

Such a feeling of rage
Under each ray of sun
Belonging to the tulips
When their decay is done.

A dull finesse of trees
Mouths the evening grief
Fruit turned to seed,
The shadows are bereaved.

Stars of gold

Swiftly in my dreams,
Rugged and forlorn,
Tasselled corn
In the velvety fields of gold
Bend in ochre bud;
Small silky spears
Lit like candles from above.

And as the locks of corn
Sway in the purple heat
My ragged dreams,
Eagle-eyed
Fly into the hottest sun
As the plush husks wave silently
Here and then gone.

Summers and winters

I stand by the tree with millions and millions
Of spangled suns awash with summer glow.
As If brimming with tumbling leaves,
Crashing into the sun's bow,
We stand like crushed apple,
Red and glorious to the taste,
Languid and ruddy in face.

In this summer-winter,
Against the paper wind
We blow like the voices of rhyme.
Dying quietly in the babbling bells
We wait,
To wait again
For all dying to cease
And wilfully close.

The muse is singing

I am tracing dandelions,
Cartwheels white as snow
As their seeds blow
To other lands
Like flickering orange sands.
Feather caps drift
Like golden spells
Small glory- fires burning, lifting,
Mottled with suns
Daring to dream.

In cotton rags she flew
In copper-blue,
Singing as if she knew
Her seeds would burst with joy
When the giddy winds blew.

The muse is singing.
In the wilderness of reverie
I am tracing dandelions
Across the candlelit sky.

The revelation of spring

In my mind's sweet dwelling
The corn is ripe and swelling,
The swallow's nest is throbbing
With yellow huddled fledglings.

The sky tears blue and rippling,
The clouds so white and drifting,
And primrose dots the streams
With twinkling starry sheen.

And as the fiery sun
Lets go her bright full gown
Love weaves to the East
The colours of sundown.

So with the fullest hope

Those childish dreams awoke

I cast my last regard

For Nature spun so wild.

And if I once forget

The pleasures of my sight

Please in some small way

Set my conscience right.

Leaves

We press to the trees

Leaves,

Like watery tattoos,

Jaded and bronzed

Telling of a mind without synchrony

or symmetry

Left behind,

Left far behind

In corners of silent loss

Where nothing is kind,

Beauty is blind

And nothing is kind

and even the leaves

Blow away.

Sea

The wave hollows circles

Like blue saucers

Out of the caves of sea

Where light drifts

Like stilted diamond

Through the caverns of spray.

Like strands of a lamp,

Sparse and unlinked

The sepia sea

Blinks,

And frothy rims, yellow like sails,

Rise and sink

In even scallops,

Grumbling shores to reach.

In Rows

You fade like tramlines
Across a Perspex sky,
Paper blotted with tears
Prints a rhyme without a reader
Were we in this tumbledown life?
Kicking coke cans across gritty fields,
Ragged lines from people's mouths,
How mad, how terribly sad we were.
You fade like tramlines,
Making tracks for me, for us,
Tracks through flowers.
And like a misty morning
Love picks her way through petals
Where chestnuts and hazelnuts grow
In rows.

Tide

The tide draws back,

The blue waves like ribbons

Line the satin sea, drifting.

Like tiny stars overturning

Shadowy peaks

Back and forth returning.

And no longer will I go searching

Tonight

Through the ribbons of satin sea,

In the cold rifts repeating,

Gentle diamonds retreating

Along the sore belt of light declining.

Watch

I wait to watch sea-green leaves

Shuffle in the wind,

Shadows.

I wait to hear the thready song

Shifting in the dulcet light,

Shadows.

I wait to hear raw, ragged trees

Glittering in between the breeze,

Shadows.

I wait to clutch the lonely hour

And turn her from her sultry glower,

Shadows.

And in a flurry of quiet nerve

I raise my wings like a throaty bird

Ready to soar into sky bluer

Than mirrored clouds passing through,

Light.

Berry

Berries glisten in the warm night air,

Plucky and swollen in the cold wind bare,

Mauve in the wonder of the stars up high

Bright as ruby dye.

The grey-bone branches wild and scratchy

Hang in woollen snow,

Numb and patchy.

Winter lies in her cold despair,

Blushing in purple, fearless glare.

Sweet the night,

Bursting and weary,

Clad in white,

Winter berry.

World

Small world,

Defined by the shadows

On the walls

By sun's white ticking dials.

Small world,

In black and white stencils

Still bright as the moon dissembles,

Yellow roses shine,

Small world

Like a flame-tree,

Ripening, rich russet fruit,

Copper, crushed dandelion

At your feet.

Rich world.

As the lilac wanes

Summer is old.

Like a rake

We pull cold leaves

From her grey-green fingers.

It is a garland of snow,

A quizzical scent of rose

That shows Age its colour.

Rainy skies still offer blushing clouds

To her rosed wildflowers,

Red-cheeked,

As if not told that she had grown old.

And in lilac June

Time appears to have forgotten her wrinkles,

So beautiful, clawing at her existence.

Blizzards

The orange blizzards,

A trauma,

Damson leaves uncover

A winter mulch.

We draw into folded snow.

The soul of darkness

Treads on light.

Rose deciphers brightness

Into an abacus.

The blizzard smoulders

Into daydreaming,

Its orange tastes bitter.

Biting pills,

Rosehips taste better.

Calculating trauma.

Breathing light

The sun in her desire

Folds the sea into pleats

Neat and reserved,

Waves of stretched blue

Like tiaras on sunny water

All this glory shimmered like crystal flutes

On the froth of ripples

In a kind of flower grey.

All this beauty lit

And all this feeling,

Dry, glimmering,

How like the sea is love-

Dogged and endlessly devoted

To herself,

Breaking her spit infinitely, gloriously,

Into the whitest of spray,

Flickering along the silent careless bay.

Clouds of honey

Honey-combe crumbles

On the roof of my tongue,

Pieces of thread, un-sown,

Untangling into the sun...

And in sizzling swarms

Like clotted fire

Honey glistens in my russet jaw

And wets my desire....

As the candy pulls gently

Into purple mists,

Like black tar my tears eclipse...

And in this blue

Like melted hyacinths

A hive of joy exists,

Dividing the skies,

Sun and rain.

I taste the heavy scent of blossom

Under my tongue,

My mouth tipped with pollen...

My eyes are wet

Imagining,

in the gaudy gold of my mind,

A breath for the trees

And peace for the clouds that shine.

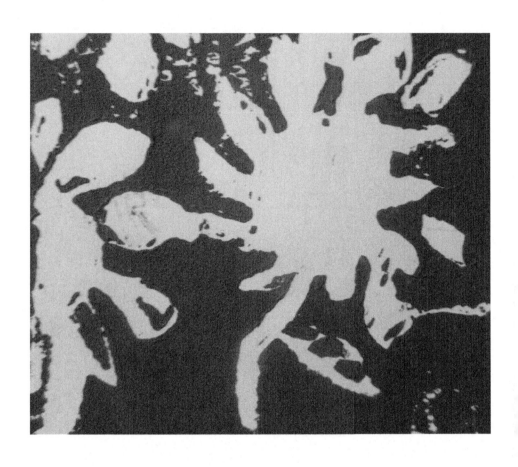

Printed in Great Britain
by Amazon